LIFE BETWEEN THE BUNS

JULIAN BERGER

ISBN: 0692223568
ISBN-13: 978-0692223567 (Julian Berger Comedy)

DEDICATION

Dedicated to all the people unaware of the douchiness in this
world. I am here for you.
—Julian Berger

Acknowledgments

I would like to thank my brother, Isaac, for his great cover illustration, my dad for supporting me, and my mother for "letting" me write this. Clearly, she hasn't read it yet. Lastly, thanks to you for reading it.

Contents

LIFE BETWEEN THE BUNS

(I'm sorry for another title page. I'll get on with the book now.)

Intro (or What Legit Books Say, Prologue)

When I decided to write a book, it seemed funny how hard it was to come up with things to write about—with the exception of what goes on in my daily life. People always say, write about what you know. So, that's why I'm going to write about my life and the funny shit I have noticed in it. Now I know you don't know me, whoever you are, but since you are one of the many millions of people reading my great literature (sarcasm), you are in for a real treat (seriously). Anyway, my name is Julian Berger, and at this very moment, I am a fifteen-year-old freshman at a public high school in Southern California. I probably shouldn't be writing this book, or whatever this turns out to be, because I have school and a basketball game tomorrow, but just the very idea that the words that I am writing down on these pages might actually get published someday…well, that is somehow inspiring me. I have many thoughts racing through my brain, as most people do. I think that most of my thoughts are sarcastic and sometimes even funny, and who knows—maybe if people actually heard them, I wouldn't be the only one laughing. So, here it goes.

Being a teenager, I have the opportunity to experience quite a lot of stupid shit. For those of you too old to remember, or not old enough yet to realize it, or maybe just completely clueless, it really does suck being this age. I'm not sure exactly when it happened, but for some reason, I spend way too much time worrying about my appearance. No, not in the way Kim Kardashian does—more like in the "why the hell do I have to worry about this shit" kind of way. Of course, I know every teenager is obsessed with the mirror. I miss the days when everyone could just be silly little elementary school kids, not caring about blah and bleh. For example, if you don't know me, and you probably don't since I'm not popular or whatever, but I have a shit ton of hair. I think it's pretty cool, but who cares what I think? Every day—and I swear I get the same comment every day—it's "When are you gonna cut your hair?" And my only response is, "Maybe when you stop asking that damn question." I mean, why the hell do you douchebags care so much about my hair anyway? It is as if they pay more attention to my hair than to a chick with a nice ass passing by…and trust me, that's much more interesting than my long hair.

So, as I started writing about my life, it hit me. The reason why high school life is so excruciatingly painful is because just about everybody and everything I encounter every day pretty much sucks. Don't believe me? Let me break it down for you.

CHAPTER 1

PEOPLE SUCK

As you can see, in the first chapter of my book (which will probably never be published), I will be talking about how people suck. I know, big generalization. *Surely you don't mean that all people suck, right, Julian?* Actually, I do. All of us suck in one way or another. Yeah, I said it. Tough shit. If you haven't noticed that people suck by now, then I recommend you read this chapter thoroughly. Now I'm not saying all people suck all the time, but the vast majority suck way too much most of the time. If you've heard the expression, "People are inherently evil," well, it's kind of like that. I mean, it's not like there is a choice here. Most assholes just haven't become self-aware enough to realize how much they suck. This is evident from the shitty, self-absorbed comments people make, to judging everybody and everything all the time. Even the rare, cool people sometimes tend to suck. It's natural. But, for the ones that just suck all the time…well, that's a different story. You see, I could go on and on and rage about how people suck like I just have for the past ten sentences, but instead, I'm going to describe some of the common personas of suckiness in something I like to call "The Douche Glossary."

The Tool

The tool is the guy who thinks he is a total chick magnet, and although he may somehow actually be attractive to some girls, what he doesn't realize is that these girls are stupid and that he is, in fact, a total cock. The tool's favorite topics of conversation consist of me, myself, and I. This person will do nearly anything to impress the girls. The tool rarely does something undouchey (new word that means not being a douche). This guy spends the majority of his days walking around without a shirt for no reason. He ends every sentence with "bro" or "dude." Just his voice alone exemplifies his inner toolness. He will dress like shit and say it is the "new style." When he is with his friends, he isn't thinking about them, which is probably fine because his tool friends aren't thinking about him either. No, they are all paying attention to the total ten walking by and formulating a plan on how to get her. Now do you know the guy I'm talking about?

The Attention Whore

We all know this fella. You know, the one always grasping for attention. I'm pretty sure the title says it all. But if you couldn't comprehend: it is someone who will do anything to get even just a little bit of attention. This could be anything from yelling in class, to wearing something unusual, or even singing out loud.

Example:

> Teacher: Okay, today in class we will—
> Attention Whore: YO, WHAT'S UP, MRS. T?
> (The caps mean yelling if you didn't catch on.)
> Everyone's thoughts: What the fuck!
> Attention Whore: LALALALALALALA.
> Me: Yep, that's an attention whore all right.

He is constantly looking around to see if his plan to get attention is working. It usually does grab other people's attention. But it just makes the attention whore look so needy, which he is. However, when it doesn't work, he goes to plan B, which is pretty ugly. Plan B is a series of even more ridiculous attempts of attention grabbing. This can be anything from jumping around to interrupting people when they are talking. Unless you can totally block out the attention whore's quest for attention, you have to acknowledge him just to get him to stop and move on to someone else. Yeah, I know, not a great solution, but at least you get him to stop. Bottom line: this person sucks and wants attention.

The Bragger

> "Just got another A-plus in AP history; no biggie."
> "Yeah, I just scored thirty points in my basketball game."

"You like my six-pack? Me too."

"Just took a ride in my new Ferrari; pretty cool if I say so myself."

Isn't that annoying? Seriously, keep this shit to yourself, you over-achieving, muscle-bound, rich, Ferrari-driving dick. I don't care. The problem is none of us say anything to stop him, so the brag-ger just keeps on bragging. It never stops. Then other people start bragging too. It spreads like an epidemic, and now I have to go to school with a bunch of fucking bragging idiots all trying to out-brag each other. My dick is bigger than yours blah, blah, blah—I don't care! (I don't understand why people say their dicks are bigger than someone else's. It's not like they have measured everyone's dick; unless they have, and they just didn't measure mine because they don't want to be embarrassed—just saying.) I mean, everyone brags a little, but this person always finds a way to plug his latest accom-plishment. But beware—this person may even throw a compliment your way just to have an excuse to reveal some great thing he did in relation to what you did.

For example, the bragger will say, "Hey, what did you get on the test?"

I'll say, "Ninety percent; you?"

He'll then say, "Oh, I got a 100 percent, pretty good, right?"

But I don't blame him. I find it interesting to learn how he hasn't missed a point in his AP physics class. (Sarcasm included if you couldn't tell.) Hey, I got a brag for you—I'm writing a book and showing how you are a complete douche.

The Kissup

This douche kisses up to practically everyone he wants on his side. The most obvious targets are coaches and teachers. I fucking hate that. The pathetic teachers are so excited and surprised for the attention that they don't even see the kissup as a kissup. This really fucks me over because I am not a kissup at all and don't ever plan on being one. Don't get me wrong. You should be nice and respectful to teachers or whoever, but not just to get them to like you or give you a better grade. The kissup will say anything just to win you over. He usually does that fake nod, smile, or even laugh to act like he is interested in you. For example, if I were to say, "I went to McDonald's yesterday," he would make it seem much more interesting than it actually is by saying, "OMG, you go to McDonald's too? It is the absolute best! Have you tried the Big Mac?" I mean, shut the fuck up! I sometimes make the shittiest jokes, and a person will laugh, leading me to conclude that he is a kissup. Kissups are basically phonies, but with a far worse title and goal.

The Held-Back Guy

Now don't get me wrong, I totally understand keeping someone in the same grade for more than one year for academic or maturity purposes. However, when it is solely for "athletic purposes," well, that's just wrong. This person thinks he is the shit because he dominates in sports and gets all the girls just because he is a *tad* bit older. Well, guess what, asshole? I could be totally unstoppable in basketball and football against a bunch of little seventh-graders, and could probably even get all the girls to like me—well, not really, but the sports for sure, unless of course there are other held-back ninth-graders. At the end of the day, I don't really hate the held-back guy as much I question his parents: What are you thinking? If you really think your kid is going to get a football scholarship, wouldn't you want to make sure he goes up against the best competition, not a bunch of little pansy-assed twelve-year-olds that haven't hit puberty yet? And held-back guy: If you really stop and think about it, don't you see how pathetic you are driving to the mall to pick up your new beard trimmer in ninth grade? You know, you really should still be a teenager when you graduate high school.

The Unnecessary Cusser

Yeah, this guy—after everything he says you hear "fuck," "shit," and so on. Trust me, I have my way with bad language on occasion too (okay, you may think I cuss a lot but that is just because I'm fucking pissed off—oh shit, not again with the cussing), but the Unnecessary Cusser takes it to a whole other level. And the funny part is that his language doesn't even make sense. Most of the time, the cusser doesn't combine the right cuss words together. Example: "My fucking shit-ass teacher sucks and always gives me a fuck-ton of homework. Her fuckface God dammit shit man what the fuck?" If you're going to cuss this much, at least be good at it or know what you're saying, you fucking nonsense-spewing, Tourette-screaming dumbass motherfucker. Fuck you!

Mr. "Correct"

This person never says or does anything wrong…well, at least from his shitty point of view. This dude will never take the blame or fault for anything, even when the evidence against him is overwhelming. For example, he will argue with anyone until that person either gives up or agrees with him that he is the smartest person on the planet. Here is an example of an awful conversation with this shitty person:

> Me: My middle name is Matthew.
> Mr. Correct: No, it's David.
> Me: No, I think I know my middle name. It's Matthew.
> Mr. Correct: Are you sure?
> Me: Yes, I'm fucking sure, you piece of shit.
> Mr. Correct: I think you're wrong. I am pretty sure it's David.
> Me: Whatever you say, douchebag.
> Mr. Correct: I knew you would see it my way.

Judge Judy

I use Judge Judy for the section heading because I think it's kind of funny (and she is the only judge I've heard of), but this person's name doesn't have to be Judy. In fact, this *judge* would probably judge and mock you if your name was Judy. I don't know why, but that is what these people do—judge, for no reason, even though nobody wants to hear it. This person has an overwhelming need to

offer his opinion and never has anything good to say. If needed, he will come up with some bullshit about you to judge.
Example:

Judge Judy: Wow, you're wearing that shirt with those shorts? Ha-ha-ha.

Me: I guess. Why, what's wrong with them?

Judge Judy: Wow, you don't even know what is wrong with that. Wow—ha-ha-ha—you are a joke.

Me: I'm sorry, but I didn't ask for your opinion, okay? And neither did the other forty people you "advised" today.

Can you believe some people get paid to judge people? I mean, like the people who will review this book (that's if it ever gets published). Also, Simon Cowell! He is a well-known, famous asshole/judge. That must be an amazing job—sitting around, cussing, acting like you know a lot about music, insulting the shitty contestants, and you're British, for God's sake. Can that get any better? Only downside of that job, though, is that you have a massive tool by the name of Ryan Seacrest as your host. (See "The Tool" section above for details.) I can't believe I just used an *American Idol* reference. Yikes! I mean, even I am judging people right now, but only because they are assholes. Now imagine how much the Judge Judys judge over random shit. It's crazy.

The Phone Person

Oh no, not this guy. I suppose the good news is at least I don't have to worry about offending phone people because they are too *busy* on their phones, and not reading my exquisite writing about how much they suck. Yeah, these people have no social skills in real life because they are too busy living life by texting on their cell phones. I know I sound old here, but there is a difference between occasionally *checking* your Instagram or whatever and constantly looking on your phone to see if Hotty_McBride posted a new hot pic. You can tell this obsessive-compulsive behavior has gone too far when you hear them using their texting language in real conversations. For example, if you say LOL, then you're obviously bullshitting because if you actually were laughing out loud, you wouldn't be saying idiotic phrases like LOL. Some people take it to a whole other level when they are on their phones and walking. Yeah, you know that slow dude in front of you texting his other douchey friends. Go on, finish your next text. I hope you and your idiot friend are having a great conversation—but in all honesty, move the fuck out of my way before I make you unable to tweet again. There should be a law against texting and walking. Seriously.

I could go on and on and add even more people to "The Douche Glossary," but then I would have a seven-hundred-page book. Who wants to read that much of my dry humor anyway? Honestly, for the few cool people you actually do come across, cherish them because they do not come around that often. Even treat the people who aren't that cool well, because, hey, at least they're not assholes.

CHAPTER 2

THESE WOMEN

Ah, women. These women. They make men's lives so hard, and no, I'm not making a penis joke, even though as a fifteen-year-old male that is my specialty. Women are so tough to understand. If women had penises, life would be much easier. Not that it would be attractive, but it would help men know if that smile is actually an "Oh, I like you" smile and not a "Get the fuck away from me" smile. I try to understand women. I truly do, but in the end, I'm completely lost.

First off, what does the word "cute" mean in the female dictionary? I used to think being called cute was something good, but I have come to realize that it is actually really, really bad. For example, when you're trying to be serious with a girl and she says, "Aww, you're so cute." Sounds good, right? But no, apparently cute is not a good thing at all in the female dictionary. And why do they have to add "aww" or anything else that sounds like a good thing but really is the exact opposite? Why do they fuck with men in the way we don't want to be fucked with? Just say "no thanks" or "not interested." Granted, that is still not the answer we want, but at least they are saying what they mean. We will be mad for a couple of minutes, and then we can go find some other hottie.

But no, these women have to put on an Oscar performance with their fake smiles, bullshit "compliments," and shitty emoji text messages. WTF ☹? Also, why do these women complain when men look at their bodies? If you want us to stop looking at you, put on some clothes so we won't be so distracted. Or you can just deal with horny men staring at you with practically no clothes on. On second thought, I can deal with a little complaining. Yeah, that sounds better. Moving on…

As hard as it is talking to or attempting to talk to girls, it's even harder texting them. You really have to choose your words carefully because you know they do. I mean, with that smiley-face bullshit and all those phony "cute" and "sweet" words, men are absolutely fucked. And by fucked, I don't mean the sexually fucked. No, I mean, "oh shit, I am being eaten by a monster" fucked. And the worst part is men are downright easy to understand, so that gives women an unfair advantage. And listen to these words very carefully: the woman always wins. Yeah, you heard me, and trust me, it hurts me to say it. But it's the damn, cold truth. For all other men hopelessly trying to understand the female species, I hope this at least was relatable since I really have no idea how to help here.

CHAPTER 3

FAMILY

You guys might be thinking, "This guy is going to make fun of family. Wow, he's one piece of work." Well, maybe I am a piece of work, but that's not going to stop me from talking about family. Don't get me wrong; I love my family more than anything. But sometimes they do stuff you just have to laugh at. I will explain why.

Parents

Just so you know I am not a complete ass, I realize that in most cases, parents are there for you every step of the way. But sometimes they are either a step behind or a couple steps too far ahead. What I mean is that sometimes they can be yelling and screaming your name constantly during your basketball game when all you want them to do is to just shut up! Other times, you look up after making the best catch of your promising football career, and they aren't even there at all. (My thoughts aren't all sports related; I'm just giving you some prime examples, so calm down.) Then there are the parents who push you too hard:

"If you don't get straight As, you are grounded!"

"You only scored ten points; come on."

"Why are you watching TV? Don't you have something to study for?"

I totally understand that you, as a parent, want your children to be the best they can be, but sometimes you guys push it way too far. Be happy that your kids give it their all or are just doing something they love. There also are the parents who can't stop talking about their honor-roll student, so much so that they even have to put a sticker on the back of their car. (Hmmm, I wonder what their child is like—maybe a bragger, don't you think? Me too.) There are also the parents who have no idea what their children are up to and could honestly not care less. I'm not saying all parents are going to be exactly how I explain them to be, but there are definitely some out there like the ones I talked about. Trust me, I have parents.

Grandparents

I know you guys might be thinking, "Old people who love you… How could you possibly make fun of them, Julian? You must be a real asshole." Well, asshole or not, I am going to continue on with this book. Now, I have categorized grandparents into four different kinds:

1. The "obsessed" grandparent. Most people like these kind of grandparents because they will practically do or buy anything for you. I don't know why or how they are so attached to their grandkids, especially when grandparents are older, but who knows? Maybe it is because they feel guilty for screwing up their own kids. Or, maybe when you reach a certain age, things just change drastically. I, for one, can't imagine myself being an obsessed grandparent since I hate everything. But hey, like I said, maybe things will change.

2. The "I don't give a shit about you" grandparents. These are the complete opposite of the obsessed grandparents. Okay, maybe they do actually care about you, but they definitely don't show it. These are the type of grandparents who give tough love or whatnot. They act like they don't want to talk to you, but hey, you probably don't want to talk to them either, especially when you become a piece-of-shit teenager. Well, you don't want to talk to them until you notice that they are some of the few people in the world who actually give a shit about you, whether they hide it or not. And trust me. It is hard to tell if the "I don't give a shit about you" grandparents actually do give a shit about you. Maybe they are just testing you, and if so, they are quite good at it.

3. The "back in my day" grandparents. They are the typical old fellas reliving the past, which I totally understand. The past sounds fun. You could do all kinds of crazy shit, except there was no Internet, which they emphasize quite a

lot. Anyway, you don't hear kids these days going on about being able to watch movies on their phone, laptop, TV, and iPad. If you have been paying attention, you know that I don't think the present is worth bragging about. And also, shouldn't they just be enjoying their retirement? Being on vacation every day doesn't seem bad to me.

4. The "hip" grandparents. These happen to be the opposite of the "back in the day" grandparents. You gotta love these guys. They try so hard to be modern and up-to-date. However, sometimes they try too hard, like extremely too hard. I mean, I for one hate all selfies in general, but I especially would hate to see the selfie disease infect the elderly. That would be way too tragic. Please, anybody but the wise elderly!

Well, that's all I've got to say about grandparents. Well, except that despite all the things I said, I, in fact, love my grandparents and will probably have to apologize to them since they are probably among the few people actually reading this book. Thanks Granny and Pop. I'm sorry for being a douche.

Siblings

It's funny—well, at least for me—that everybody who is an only child wants a brother or sister, and everyone who has a sibling wants him or her gone. Anyway, let me tell you what I think about siblings. I think they are made to be your enemy. Everything is a competition. And you are surprised when they do something nice. I honestly don't know what happens when you grow up and how you suddenly become friendly with them. Maybe it's the fact that you don't live in the same house anymore. Or maybe it's because you don't have to get dragged to their six-hour track meets anymore. (Trust me, those are a bitch.) It also may be that you have an epic battle when you are older, and after that, you both sign a peace treaty. I don't know, but I do know if there is a war of the siblings, I will be prepared. Whatever the reason may be, somehow you still love that person who punches you at random times.

Cousins

These relatives can be either your best friends or complete strangers. For cousins, I don't have much to make fun of mostly because they are such a random and difficult family member to talk about. I know, big shocker. But hey, I still got something. For those of you who aren't tight with your cousins, what do you talk about? Mandy's Bat Mitzvah? Uncle Jeff's Prius? I mean, there is a significant shortage of topics to choose from. Also, what if you are complete opposites, and they are basically like the creepy guy or girl who sits next to you in class? That could be a nightmare, especially if you have to pretend to be *friendly* with them. And what if they are one of the many people I described in the Douche Glossary? I mean, this could be really bad. Hopefully, you are on the same page with your cousins and aren't complete enemies or strangers with them. Good thing I lucked out.

Nephews/Nieces

Listen, I don't have any nephews/nieces, but I assume they're just like sons or daughters, except you are even less interested in them and have even less in common. It must be awful trying to start conversations with them, pretending like you're interested and shit. Unless, of course, they are teenage comedians like me. But hey, it must be as bad for them as it is for you. Maybe that's what you two should talk about.

Example:

> You: I have no idea what to say to you, so I'm just going to pretend I'm interested in everything you say.
> Nephew/Niece: Same here. I didn't even know your name until my dad told me today.
> You: Okay, glad we are on the same page.

Aunts/Uncles

These guys are basically like another set of parents. Yeah, doesn't sound like a really good title. I mean, who really needs another set of parents these days? Parents already hound you for practically everything and are so attached…except for me, since they are letting me write this important piece of literature. (Or are they? At this point in time, I still don't know if this book will ever see the light of day.) Aunts and uncles act super nice to us since we are not their children and they don't know our ugly side. And we really think they're awesome since they are not really our parents and we don't know their ugly side. We don't know what they do to their own children, and they don't know what we do to our real parents. Both just assume that the other is the greatest person ever, so we treat each other like that. However, the moment they find your dark side or you find theirs, everything changes. (Yes, people, we all have dark sides. Get over it.) In the end, everyone likes being treated as the greatest person ever. I mean, seriously, who doesn't?

CHAPTER 4

Teachers/Coaches

I **know you guys** are probably wondering why I would combine teachers and coaches in one chapter. Well, if you look at it like I do, they are both people who are "there for you" and are not important enough to have their own chapters. (Or in other words, I'm just too lazy.)

Teachers

I know that teachers are here to help people learn and yada, yada, yada. But let's be real here. Can they possibly do it in some sort of interesting way? And no, "interesting" doesn't mean crappy jokes found on the back of a cereal box or a five-minute educational animation video from the 1970s. It also doesn't mean an educational "song." I didn't sign up for chorus for a reason. Also, no more art projects in math class. There is an actual art class for that shit. I'm not just saying no to art projects because I suck at art, but because they usually don't relate to the class *at all*. Stick to the subject, but make it somewhat interesting so I won't fall asleep. (Because, you know, I'd much rather learn than take a nap.) Also, don't say: "I don't want to give you homework." We both know that is complete bullshit. If you honestly didn't want to give us homework, I wouldn't have any *ever*, especially on spring break.

Coaches

Every coach says the same thing: "All I care about is effort." That's awesome, and I respect that. Except most of the time it's not entirely true. Gasp. Yeah, I know, crazy, right? A coach lying? What? Unbelievable! Yep, they'll just accuse you of not working hard enough and use it as an excuse to take you out of the game. How do they know how hard I am working? Just because I mess up on a play doesn't mean that I am not trying hard. Now that's not always the case, but it tends to happen quite often. And if you really want our attention and respect, yelling isn't always the way to go. Look at it like this: kids respect their parents the most, and most likely parents don't give them shit or yell at every little mistake they make. So maybe you should act more like parents? Oh my God, what am I saying? I don't know. It kind of sounds good to me. I'm not saying not to yell when people aren't paying attention or are goofing off, but still, you don't have to yell constantly. JUST STOPPPPP! (That was a yell if you didn't notice.) But what the hell do I know? I'm just a "stupid teenager."

CHAPTER 5

SCHOOL

Let's be real: school sucks, and it always will. Nobody wants to learn, nobody wants to do work (especially when you are not getting paid to do so), and nobody wants to have annoying teachers command them. But we still do it anyway because, you know, education is "the building blocks to success." Now I will break down each school individually and tell you why they suck.

Preschool

Is this even a school? You don't have to think or do anything, so I don't think it is. I think it is just an excuse to meet annoying people the same age as you. Also this "school" has nap time, which nobody likes at age four. Too bad we don't get to take naps in high school and middle school when we actually want them. Preschool should just focus on teaching kids not to be douchebags. But instead they just pile on the art projects. Yeah, that sounds like school, full of complete bullshit.

Elementary School

Elementary school is a blast, yet everyone is so busy picking their noses that they don't enjoy it as much as they should. You practically spend the same amount of time at recess as you do actually learning. Elementary kids do so little in class that they don't even need the breaks. They need the breaks in middle school and high school, where you actually are forced to do pointless projects and shit. Can the school board just balance out the timing of breaks and work? Maybe board members don't think breaks should be evenly dispersed because they didn't go to school.

Middle School

Middle school should not exist. It is awful, just straight-up awful. It is where all the bad shit that can happen happens. Puberty, stress, girl problems, you name it. Middle school = HELL. I honestly don't know how I made it out alive, nor will I question and think about it. I can't think of anything worse than middle school (even though I'm writing a whole book about stuff that sucks), but still, middle school is the worst. They make you actually do stuff in PE and actually grade you on PE shit. Not everyone is a "#D1Bound athlete". (This means a really good athlete if you didn't know.) Anyone can work hard and study in school, but not everyone can run a mile in under eight minutes or climb a giant rope. Oh, and this is when people start to suck and start to fall into the various types of people I mentioned earlier in The Douche Glossary. All in all, middle school = HELL.

High School

Only been here one year and can see that it is basically the same shit as middle school except:

(+ means good and - means bad)

More work	-
Hotter girls	+
More competition	-
More pressure	-
Less free time	-
Costs more money for extracurricular activities	-
Douchier people	-

That is pretty much it. School is still the same old, same old. I'm also sad to say that every clichéd high school movie with the douchebag getting the girl is true, except for the part when the good guy finally gets the girl in the end. That doesn't happen—*trust me*.

College

Haven't been there yet, but I've heard plenty of stories from people who like bragging about it. "Those college days, man, they were wild, and I mean *wild*." I also know that it costs a shit ton, and I mean a *shit ton* of money to go to one. And before that, you have to get accepted in order to pay the shit ton of money. It sounds like society doesn't want people going to college, which is funny because don't we want more employed people? In order to get a decent job, you need a college degree, so shouldn't they maybe, uh, lower the prices?

CHAPTER 6

STEREOTYPES

Most people stereotype other people the minute they see them. It comes naturally. When people see a tall, African American (fancy word for black dude), they automatically think, "Shit, this guy is going to be one hell of an athlete." Why? Why do we think that? When people sit on a comfortable black couch one time, they don't automatically think the next time they see a black couch, "Oh, this is going to be comfortable. I sat in a comfortable one last week, so this must be exactly the same." I don't understand why some Caucasians (fancy word for white people) make fun of these stereotypes, especially when their stereotypes include being nonathletic and uncool. Of course, white people think they are the "normal" race to which every other race is compared. But what is normal, anyway? You know what I mean, nobody thinks they speak with an accent either. From your own perspective, you speak "normally." As a white person, having the African American or Asian stereotype actually seems way better than having the boring white one. Not that stereotypes are good, but still, being white is just not that interesting. Asians and African Americans get to be thought of as smart or athletic, while white is just, well, white. I imagine that if I was black, I wouldn't think that I was super athletic, just that everyone else was not athletic. Also, if I was Asian, I wouldn't think I was super smart or anything, just that everyone else was a complete dipshit. You see, it is really all perspective. Better yet, why have stereotypes at all? Would it be so hard to just treat everyone equally, and not make inferences about people just because of the way they look? Yeah, let's just do that and not be a bunch of pre-judging douchebags.

CHAPTER 7

Social Media

Social media is all anybody talks about these days. Excuse me, *tweets* about these days. I know what you're thinking: Why would a fifteen-year-old complain about social media when he probably uses it? Well, I do use some forms of social media, but that doesn't mean I actually like them, which I don't. I know this chapter will probably make me sound like an old man, but hey, at least it doesn't make me look like a self-absorbed douchebag, like most of the people who tweet constantly and post selfies on Instagram. Now instead of combining all forms of social media into one, big cluster-fuck, I'm going to individually break down why each and every one of them sucks.

Instagram

Don't get me wrong, I like quality pictures. But sadly, it's very rare to find any good pics on this app. Instead, you will find over a million selfies of people who like themselves way too much. Whoever created the selfie phenomenon must've been the most stuck-up, self-absorbed douche to ever live. I mean really, stop taking pictures of yourself in those weird poses. What do you honestly think you are getting from these shitty and awkward photos? Attention? (See Attention Whore above) I guess you kind of are, but definitely not the good kind of attention. The line of shitty pictures doesn't stop there. No, you will see random quotes that have nothing to do with the photos above them. Oh, and *hashtags* don't make this app any better. I don't know who came up with the idea of hashtags either, but it has to be the most random and biggest joke ever (#WTF). Why hashtags? Why not a star or a plus sign before every phrase? I'm just saying a star would be pretty cool. But hashtags—just random. Anyway, maybe if people weren't so self-absorbed, this app wouldn't be such an atrocity. Then again, if that were the case, maybe nobody would ever post anything.

Twitter

I honestly don't know why people think that other people care that they "just finished practice" or "can't believe it's summer." I mean, I don't care, and I'm guessing nobody else does. If you wouldn't say this random shit out loud, why would you write it where anyone can see it? Some people don't even make sense with their vague tweets. For example, "How could you do this to me?" Who are you talking about, and why are you sharing this with everybody else in the world when we clearly don't understand what the fuck you're saying? Did you ever hear of e-mail or texting? Honestly, everybody's tweets suck, but if you must do it, at least have them make sense or not be an inside joke or story. The only reason I tweet is to (a) make fun of Twitter, and (b) make fun of the stupid shit in the world, just like what I'm doing in this book. Wow, I sound like a great guy to follow (@TheJulianBerger).

Facebook and Myspace

Nobody uses these, so there is really nothing to complain about except for the annoying parents writing about their "amazing," "God-gifted" children. I'm talking about Facebook for the parents; nobody is on Myspace, not even the people who created it.

Vine

Other than the few creative people who actually make funny videos, the typical people on Vine suck. Taking selfies is bad enough, but videos of random people staring and making weird faces at the camera aren't entertaining, just freaky. Adding shitty music to someone else's video or copying someone else's vine won't win you fans either. Go to YouTube for some actual quality videos that aren't over after you blink and don't repeat endlessly. (Why not also subscribe to me on YouTube—julianbergercomedy.)

Snapchat

If you're looking for slutty pictures and even more selfies that last for just ten seconds, then Snapchat is the app for you. Yeah, that's pretty much what the app is. Oh wait, you can also have videos—even better. You know the pictures suck if they disappear after ten seconds. I'm sad to say it, but this makes Instagram seem like an amazing app. That was hard to write.

I'm sure there are plenty of other shitty social media networks that suck, but I haven't had the chance to experience them to find out exactly why they suck. So you are stuck with only five rants. I know you wanted more, but there are still many more chapters. Don't worry.

CHAPTER 8

TECHNOLOGY

Technology. It brings out the "lazy" in everyone. I know you might be thinking, "How does technology reveal our laziness?" Well, I'll tell you. I'm not saying making new technology shows people's laziness. No, it is the reason why we make technology that tells all. Why do you think we make cars and other transportation? Because nobody wants to walk—lazy. Why do you think we have movies and TV? So we don't have to entertain ourselves—lazy. Why do you think we make automatic toothbrushes? So we don't have to physically brush our own damn teeth—lazy. I mean, moving your arm up and down to brush your teeth, ooh, tiring. Why do you think we make video games? So we don't actually have to exert any physical energy whatsoever. This way, we don't have to play real basketball ourselves or shoot people in real life (which, by the way, you shouldn't do)—lazy. Why do you think we make computers? So we don't need to figure out the answer to the stupid questions we come up with—lazy. Why do you think we make cell phones, e-mail, and other communication devices? So we don't actually have to talk to people in real life—lazy. Why do you think we make social networks? So we don't need have one-on-one conversations. Now you can post your pictures and brag to everyone in one shot—lazy. And douchey—don't brag. Why do you think we make treadmills? So we don't need to physically go outside and walk—lazy. Why do you think we make Nooks, Kindles, and whatever other electronic book things? So we don't actually have to go to the bookstore and buy the damn book—lazy. If you didn't catch anything out of that, let me summarize. Technology = lazy.

CHAPTER 9

COMMERCIALS

I don't know why companies have to make such random commercials. Unless the goal is to make their product/company look dumb, these ads are not succeeding. Progressive Insurance is probably the worst because that lady in the white lab coat is scary as shit. You know who I'm talking about. Don't act like you don't. That pale, overuse-of-makeup-looking freak. If she were actually funny, skilled, or somewhat related to insurance, it would be fine, but no, it's just random and scary as shit. Why would I want to buy insurance from a freaky lady in a weird white world where bad puns are accepted?

Speaking of insurance, why would I want to buy it from a gecko, a pig, or a caveman? C'mon, Geico. I know Geico sort of sounds like gecko, but if you are going to use the gecko this much, why not change the company name to Gecko? There is no harm; it would just make sense now. And why is the gecko Australian? Can we have any backstory to this shit? Actually, I'm kind of interested in how he got into the insurance business. That story alone is a great commercial.

Then you have the beer commercials that make alcohol seem like the best thing ever, even though in little print at the bottom they say, "Drink responsibly," as if they are saying, "We want you to buy a lot, but if you die from alcohol poisoning or a car crash, don't come blaming us because we warned you, in very fine print at the bottom corner. You should have spotted that." I wonder why they warn us. Maybe because someone died from drinking too much alcohol, which led to the beer companies realizing that people thought buying their beer would lead to meeting hot girls at a beach or to a train coming on a hot day and making it snow, when it actually just leads to being drunk. I think it's crazy how these companies know people can die, get arrested, or get injured by drinking too much beer, yet all they do to prevent that is add "Please drink responsibly" in a font I'm pretty sure is called "unseen." I'm sure they could do just about anything else and it would be more effective in preventing deaths. Here's an idea, why not make the font a little BIGGER? Also, I'm pretty sure people don't pay enough attention to the beer to care if it is "straight from the Rockies." I think they would care more that the beer they drink was not a part of a shitty commercial.

And for all the car commercials—yikes! Why have all these stunts and shit in your ad and then say, "Please do not try any of the stunts at home"? Do you really think we are that stupid? And is your car really that dull that you have to make it seem like you too could do cool stunts if you drove this car?

And for Viagra and all the other similar boner drugs, I think I'd rather never get an erection again than die, go blind, or fall into a coma. But hey, that's just me. I'm sure for some people boners are far more important than eyesight or any other of the million side effects.

Oh, and for movie trailers—I honestly don't care what *Time* magazine raves. If I did, I would probably buy *Time*.

CHAPTER 10

RAP

Now don't get me wrong, I love me some sick beats. (That sounds so white. Shit, that's a stereotype. I'm a total douche.) But some of the shit on the radio is just dead awful. Especially rap. The majority of the lyrics today just suck ass. You are not good at making lyrics if you are rhyming "bitch" with "bitch" every line. Of course they rhyme; they are the same fucking word! Also, why does every song have to be about sex? I know we all think about it and like it, but come on, make a song about something else for a change. Speaking of great lyrics (*sarcasm*), 2 Chainz, what the hell are you doing? "She got a big booty so I call her big booty." Wow, I applaud you for your profound lyrics; well done. I thought I understood what music was before I heard you, but I was dead wrong. But seriously, you can't come up with anything else? If you are getting millions off that line, I think I should pursue the rap game. "She got a nice face so I call her nice face." Also, what is with everybody saying their name in every fucking song? Are you seriously that self-absorbed that you need to mention your name in every song? I know I am listening to your music because it sounds like shit. I don't need any hints. And Rick Ross, stop barking. My dogs even find it annoying, and they like to bark. Trust me.

CHAPTER 11

Politics

Being fifteen, it wouldn't seem like I know a lot about politics, which happens to be right because I don't constantly watch CNN or whatever other boring channels that broadcast political news. However, I know enough to see that politics are stupid, and I'll tell you why. First off, people are arguing over pointless shit, which makes them look stupid. The two parties arguing over the government and other shit I don't care about are equivalent to two six-year-olds fighting over a toy. Why can't the Republicans and the Democrats—I don't know—maybe stop bitching at each other and come to an agreement or compromise of some sort? I suppose their arguing is actually good for TV news networks, like CNN and Fox News, because without it, no one would ever watch them (not like anyone does). Honestly, I'm not a Republican or a Democrat. (However, even though I may have some beliefs that are more aligned with one of the parties, I don't feel the need to share, unlike the people who have stickers on their car's bumper.) I'm Julian Danger Berger, and I can't stand seeing grown men and women fighting over pointless government topics (which the average person has no idea about). I can't believe only a few people, such as Jon Stewart and Stephen Colbert, can see this. Also, what is with the elephant and the donkey? They sound like really bad WNBA teams.

CHAPTER 12

RELIGION

Oh no, this guy is talking about religion? Yikes! Yeah, I know, why would anyone bother reading about some fifteen-year-old's views on religion? *God only knows.* Now if you didn't know (which you probably don't), I'm Jewish. Yeah, yeah, big-nose jokes and penny jokes—really clever and funny. However, I do not celebrate anything hard-core or go to temple and other shit. I really just try to enjoy life with the annoying people around me.

Anyway, I think religion can do a lot of harm to the world. And I know what you're thinking: "Oh my, he hates God, yada, yada, yada." No, that's not it at all. I'm perfectly fine with people believing in whatever they want. You know, whatever makes them happy, as long as it doesn't hurt anybody. But I get pissed when people make fun of other religions or give people shit just because they believe in different things. I mean, I get mocked because I'm Jewish, and we're not even the ones who believe a super-old, fat, chimney-sliding, cookie-eating guy delivers presents by flying all over the world on a sled all in one night. I know I am mocking now as well, but c'mon, really? (Just kidding; calm down. I'm sure Santa is a great guy. I mean, he is giving out free stuff, for *God's sake*.) (Pun intended)

But seriously, think of all the deaths and wars religion has caused over the course of human history. I mean, that shit is crazy. People basically wage these big wars over their different beliefs. That's like if all the Eagles fans and me (yeah, I'm from Philly—deal with it) fight against the Cowboys fans. Do you see how stupid that would be? Yet, people fight and kill each other over their beliefs. I'm glad religion can give people happiness, but if people could just keep their beliefs to themselves, maybe the world wouldn't be so full of fighting and other crazy shit (and assholes). Some people even share their favorite excerpts or whatever from the Bible on their Instagram profiles. I mean, who gives a shit? I'm sorry but you don't see me writing on page 54: "Moses talks to a bush." And what is it with everyone thanking God when they have success? You think God gives a shit about your winning the Super Bowl? No! He is too busy sitting on the clouds, drinking wine, and sleeping with beautiful women. Well, at least that is what I think he is doing, if he is even real. (I'm just kidding.) Thank him if you want, but you can give yourself some credit too. Also, why do most people believe in God's existence, yet we don't have any evidence? But we don't believe aliens exist even though space is huge and we have only traveled to the moon. I'm just saying this shit doesn't add up. And if any of you are offended by anything I just said, I certainly didn't mean it. Just sharing my beliefs since, you know, it is my book. Just saying. It's kind of like my own religion. I'll call it *Not Being a Douchebag-ism.*

CHAPTER 13

Holidays

Holidays, celebrations, whatever. The only thing people truly celebrate is having a free day off from school or work. If the holiday doesn't give people a free day, then nobody gives a shit. Some people get really into the holiday spirit or whatever, but mostly people are just celebrating being able to sleep in. Now I am going to break down various holidays and explain why most of them suck too.

Birthdays

Trust me, I love getting gifts once a year, but I just don't understand why I get them. I didn't do anything. I just came out of my mom (sorry, bad image, I know, but it needed to be written). If anyone should be receiving gifts, it's my mom and my dad for watching this most likely disgusting scene. Not only do you get gifts, but you have to make it into some big party with food and entertainment and whatever pointless shit you can think of. I mean, you didn't win the Nobel Prize or the Super Bowl, so shut up. Remember you were born this day and don't make a big deal of it. Even if you think this is worth celebrating, why would you want to celebrate getting older? You are basically celebrating the reduction of days/years you have left in your life. If anything, birthdays are kind of depressing.

Thanksgiving

To be real, I actually love this holiday. (I know, shocking right?) You get to eat a shit ton of food, sleep a lot, watch football, and not get in trouble for doing so. How could anyone hate this holiday? If I like this holiday, I can't imagine anyone else not liking it. (I'm kidding; I'm not that big of a douche.) My only complaint is that we only get to eat this much food once a year. We should be feasting like this all the time. It's not like America is obese or anything, so why not? But seriously, Thanksgiving is probably the best holiday ever and should get more recognition. I think we should have a holiday celebrating how amazing Thanksgiving truly is. I shall call it, "Thank you, Thanksgiving Day."

Halloween

Another great holiday—well, at least for half the population. When I'm older, I will probably hate having strangers come to my house for candy. No, buy your own damn candy. We should make it so people go trick-or-treating to markets or candy stores and ask for free candy. Don't have people go to random people's houses and ask for candy. That is disrespectful and, when you think about it, stalkerish. (Yeah, I know, another made-up word; deal with it, Microsoft Word.) How come nobody has questioned this strange activity of getting candy from random people, especially when no one really even knows why they are doing it? I still don't even understand what Halloween is about, other than knocking on strangers' doors dressed like idiots and begging for candy.

Christmas

The ultimate holiday, or at least I assume. I don't know the full-on Christmas experience since I'm Jewish, but it seems pretty cool. Getting presents from a weird, fat stranger at night sounds great. Anytime you get presents for practically doing nothing is always a good time, so I doubt I could complain about the holiday if I were Christian. But since I am Jewish, I have a different view. First of all, it seems just a little over the top, don't you think? Now that I think about it, a weird, fat stranger giving me presents is kind of scary. I think I'd rather find out that my lying parents were giving the presents to me. Also, I wouldn't really dig the whole sitting on the lap of a fat stranger who actually does exist.

Hanukkah

Another holiday that involves getting presents for doing nothing. Well, at least I don't have to do anything. Yes, being the complete opposite of a hardcore Jew enables me to get all the good stuff of the religion—this being food and presents—while not doing the prayers and stuff. (I'm not saying the hardcore stuff is unimportant. I'm just not that religious and I like the food and gifts.) This is even better than Christmas, well, at least in my opinion, since you get presents for eight straight days—yes, eight straight days, *God damn.* How awesome is that, especially compared with a fat stranger coming into your house? And not to brag, we Jews don't have to sing annoying carols or make it seem like our holiday is the only one that exists in December. I know I sound biased toward Hanukkah, but I'm really not. I respect all religions equally but just dislike when people sing shitty songs, make it seem like everyone has the same religion they have, and call their religion the "normal" one. Anyway, eight straight days of presents is legit, and you should try it sometime.

Saint Patrick's Day

I completely hate this holiday. Okay, hate may be too strong a word, so let me explain. Why do people think they can pinch me just because I'm not wearing green? Seriously? That is so annoying. I don't celebrate the holiday, so back the fuck off, or I will punch you for assuming that everyone has to participate. Other than wearing green and getting drunk, I don't really get the celebration of Saint Patrick's Day. I also don't know how leprechauns relate to anything Christian or Irish, but what the hell do I know? I'm Jewish for *God's sake* (Pun intended again).

Easter

All I can think of for Easter is that it is the random celebration of giant bunnies hiding eggs. I take that back. Actually, I also think about chocolate bunnies and all the other Easter candy, good stuff. I'm pretty sure this holiday is about Christ and his resurrection, but I still don't get why that has anything to do with giant rabbits. And no, I'm not going to research to see if the rabbit has anything to do with the resurrection because that would mess up my comedy routine, so back off.

Fourth of July

Probably the worst name for a holiday since it is the date of the day, but hey, that pretty much sums up America for you guys. I know you might be sitting there thinking, "Hey, this holiday is also called Independence Day, so it isn't the worst name for a holiday." You may think you have a good point, but I doubt that anyone refers to the Fourth of July as Independence Day. I may be wrong, but still…I'm right. (and I am not being Mr. Correct here, trust me, I'm always right) Just saying, we Americans are ignorant and most people don't even actually know what happened on this day. All we know is there is going to be a shit ton of party supplies with red, white, and blue on them and fireworks for twenty minutes. Aside from that, though, what is there on the Fourth of July other than your annoying neighbors having a loud-ass barbeque?

I know I missed out on a bunch of holidays, but who do you think I am? I'm not even guaranteed this book is getting published, and you expect me to write more? *Sheesh.* And I doubt that anyone would want to hear my complaints about Passover, if you even know what that is.

CHAPTER 14

I Suck

I know you guys are probably shocked. You thought I would just rant about everything in the world and act like I am perfect; well, you've got the wrong idea. I'm not that guy who shoots a bullet but then can't take one. (Nice metaphor, right? If that even is one.) Yes, in order to make me seem like less of an asshole and tell you the truth like I have throughout the book, I will tell you why I suck. This might be hard to do. (I'm kidding; calm down.) First off, I am currently writing a book on why the world and everything in it sucks. Also, I'm super shy and can barely talk in front of people, and yet I want to be a comedian (wow, I sound like an oxymoron). I also think I can get this book published, which is highly doubtful. I am unattractive, which is most likely why I have so many failures with women. (I know, big shocker. You guys all thought I was a pimp.) I play a whole lot of video games (almost too much—*almost*). I am incredibly lazy therefore I use technology even though I just told you why it sucks. Oh shit, I also just realized that after writing this book I am an Unnecessary Cusser. But who the fuck cares?

Listen, I can go on and on about how I suck, but as long as you get the point, which I hope you do, (I mean, I gave you fourteen chapters; how much more do you need?) everything sucks, even you. And the moment you can accept the fact that you suck, you will not be the standard asshole.

Thanks for reading and surviving through this rant fest, if you did. The bottom line of this book (figuratively and physically) is that people suck, women suck, religion sucks, social media sucks, family sucks, teachers and coaches suck, politics sucks, commercials suck, rap sucks, school sucks, technology sucks, holidays suck, stereotypes suck, and I suck. Everything *sucks*. And since everything sucks, life can sometimes feel like something between the buns, and I'm not talking about a burger.

Your teenage comedian,

Julian Berger

Made in the USA
San Bernardino, CA
11 November 2014